ANTIQUITY DEPICTED

ASPECTS OF ARCHAEOLOGICAL ILLUSTRATION

THIS IS THE TENTH OF THE
WALTER NEURATH MEMORIAL LECTURES
WHICH ARE GIVEN ANNUALLY EACH SPRING ON
SUBJECTS REFLECTING THE INTERESTS OF
THE FOUNDER
OF THAMES AND HUDSON

THE DIRECTORS WISH TO EXPRESS
PARTICULAR GRATITUDE TO THE GOVERNORS AND
MASTER OF BIRKBECK COLLEGE
UNIVERSITY OF LONDON
FOR THEIR GRACIOUS SPONSORSHIP OF
THESE LECTURES

ANTIQUITY
DEPICTED

ASPECTS OF
ARCHAEOLOGICAL
ILLUSTRATION

STUART PIGGOTT

with 43 illustrations

THAMES AND HUDSON

Printed in Great Britain by
BAS Printers Limited, Over Wallop, Hampshire
Bound in Great Britain by Webb & Sons

The ninth Walter Neurath Memorial Lecture, Renaissance Fortification by J. R. Hale,
was incorrectly numbered as the eighth on its title pages.

It was twenty years ago, and appropriately enough at Stonehenge during Professor Atkinson's and my excavations, that Walter Neurath invited me to take part in an adventurous new departure in archaeological popularization which resulted in 1961 in the appearance of The Dawn of Civilization *under the Thames and Hudson imprint. But this was not all, for it began a friendship with a remarkable man which has meant much to me. Today I have been honoured by the Governors and Master of Birkbeck College in their invitation to join that select group of scholars who for the past nine years have paid tribute to his memory in an annual lecture. I have chosen a subject which I think Walter Neurath, as a student not only of art history but of prehistory under Oswald Menghin in Vienna, and with a lifetime dedicated to the depiction of Antiquity, would have enjoyed. I offer it here in his memory as a token of admiration and affection.*

IN THE FIRST MINUTE-BOOK of the Society of Antiquaries of London, in 1717, William Stukeley, its first Secretary, wrote: 'Without drawing or designing the Study of Antiquities or any other Science is lame and imperfect.' I would like to look at some of the ways in which earlier antiquaries have seen the past and put it on record.[1]

In any inquiry into visual depiction one cannot better begin than by turning to the studies of one of my eminent predecessors in these lectures, Sir Ernst Gombrich. He, with Professor Richard Gregory, has made us aware of the complex interactions of eye, brain and what A. E. Housman called 'the frailties and aberrations of the human mind, and of its insubordinate servants, the human fingers', which combine to produce an illustration. Sir Ernst has argued that a pictorial representation 'is not a faithful record of a visual experience but the faithful construction of a relational model. Neither the subjectivity of vision nor the sway of conventions need lead us to deny that such a model can be constructed to any required degree of accuracy. What is decisive here is clearly the word "required". The form of a representation cannot be divorced from its purpose and the requirements of the society in which the given visual language gains currency.'[2]

Those concerned with illustrating antiquities, which might be monuments in the field, from neolithic to Gothic, or portable objects ranging from works of art to brutish chipped stones, had over the centuries changing requirements of accuracy, and were certainly affected by the sway of conventions. Their visual schemes were often dependent on the degree of understanding they could bring to their subject; and, throughout, the question of original observation as opposed to copying may bedevil us.

7

JOHN CONSTABLE, Stonehenge, watercolour (detail), 1835

1 Merlin erecting the stones of Stonehenge; from a fourteenth-century romance

To illustrate some of the circumstances, let us look at the earliest representations of the monument of Stonehenge. There are at least two medieval representations of the monument, both of the fourteenth century. One, in a British Library manuscript [1], is anecdotal, illustrating the legend which first appeared in Geoffrey of Monmouth's *Historia* of about 1136, of Merlin re-erecting on Salisbury Plain the stones he had brought by magic from Ireland. The essentials of massive squared uprights and lintels are depicted – as they are in the contemporary view, without figures, in a manuscript in Corpus Christi College, Cambridge [2], where the circle has been squared to suit the exigencies of space. Both could well have been drawn from verbal description rather than from a direct pictorial representation. By the

8

2 View of Stonehenge, from a fourteenth-century
manuscript of the history of the world ▷

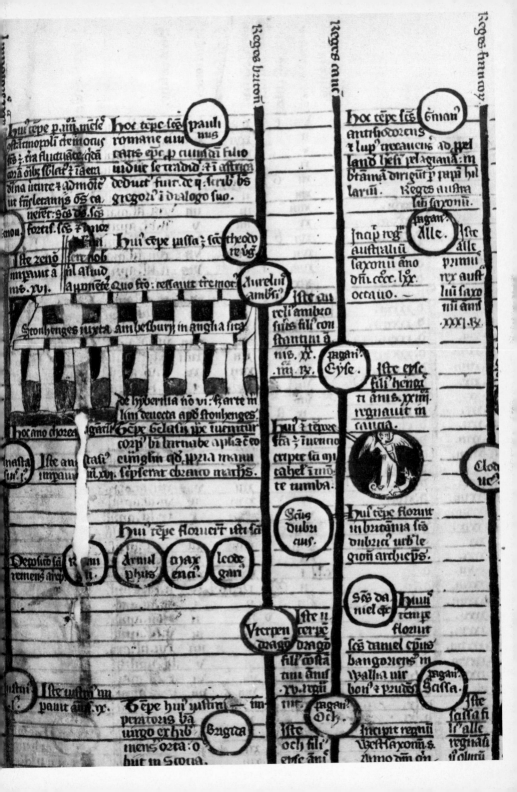

Hui tepe p̄ in miē stantinopoli tremoꝰ q̄da fluctuate: q̄da uñā uince: 7 admotē ut tñ lecarnꝰ os ea neuit: sc̄s dō. sc̄s fortis. sc̄s 7 ymor...

Iste zeno impaut̃ a ms· xvi·

Hoc tepe sc̄s paulinus romane ciui catis epc̄· ꝓ cuiusda filio uidue se tradidit: 7 ī astrictū deduct̃ fuit: de q̄ scrib̄ bs gregori̅ i dialogo suo.

Paulinus

Hui tepe passa ꝫ sc̄s theodore uirꝫ

Ameriete Quo sc̄: restaurt̃ tremoꝛ

Aurelius ambr̄

Iste aureli ambro sius fili con stantini ꝫ nus· xx· iiij· R·

Hoc tepe sc̄s germanꝰ antissiodorensis 7 lupꝰ trecauēsis ad pel land hesi pelagiana: ī brītania dirigūt ꝓ papā hil larium.   Reges austra lii saxonū.

Inap̃ reg austaliū saxonū āno dn̄i· cccc· lxx· octaũo·

Ella

Allē

Iste allē pimꝰ rex aust lii saxo nū ānū xxxi· R·

Stonhenges iuxta ambesbury in anglia sita

de hybernia no ui: karte in lili deuecta apꝺ stonhenges

Hoc ano choreā gigātꝰ   Gepe belaui ipe iuentūr corpꝰ bi barnabe apr̄z 7 co cūglm eiꝰ appria manu sepiserat ebranco marths.

Cyse

Iste epc̄ fili hengi sti ānus· pimꝰ regnauit in cantia·

Hui z tepe sca ꝫ iuento cerpte sū mi cahel i mō te tumba.

Hui tepe floruit in britania sc̄s dubricius urb le gion archiepc̄·

Scs dubri cius·

Iste anastasiꝰ fiu·i· impaut̃ in xxvii.

Anastasi...

Clod uẽ

Hui tepe flouerit isti sñ

Dewsuo sñ remens archepc̄...

druni phus   ayax ena   leode gari

Sc̄s da niel ec̄

Hui tepe floruit sc̄s daniel epc̄ bangorensis in wallia uir bon̄ 7 pɹudẽs

Iste !! cerpe dɹago fili cōsta tini ānus· xv· rex.

Vterpen drago

Iste ill̄ mꝰ paut̃ aus̅ xx·

Gepe hui ustiñ imꝑatoꝛis ba uirgo cr̄ hib mens orta: o hut in Scoia.

Bugica

pagan̄ Ocht

Iste och fili epc̄ ānus...

incipit regnū West Saxonū. ā ānno dn̄i dñ...

pagan̄ Sissa

Iste sissa fi li·alle regnaui

sixteenth century, however, when our next Stonehenge drawing appears, we have moved into a world in which topographical and landscape draughtsmanship was becoming increasingly commonplace, and into a mood of scientific sophistication in which a structure could be viewed not from the obvious eye-height level, but in the form of an artificial projection from an assumed vantage-point, the better to show detail. The iconography of Stonehenge in this form seems to go back to a Dutch pen-and-wash drawing by Lucas de Heere, dated 1574; to an engraving initialled R.F. of a year later; and to another pen-and-wash drawing of 1588 by William Smith [3], Rouge Dragon in the College of Arms, for his unpublished *Particuler Description of England*. This last is usually assumed to copy the R.F. print, but may represent an independent tradition, as topographers were around drawing megalithic monuments at first hand, as did George Owen for his *History of*

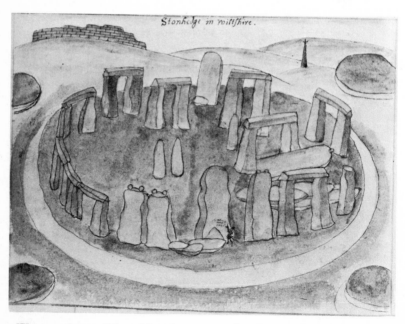

3 WILLIAM SMITH, View of Stonehenge, 1588, from his unpublished *Particuler Description of England*

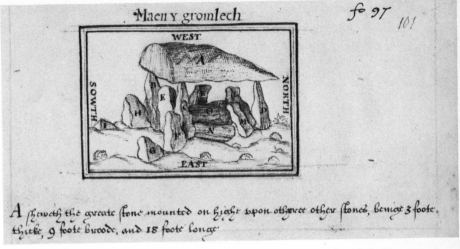

WEST

SOWTH

NORTH

EAST

A sheweth the greate stone mounted on hight upon other other stones, beinge 3 foote thicke, 9 foote broode, and 18 foote longe

4 GEORGE OWEN, Chamber tomb of Pentre Ifan, from his *History of Pembrokeshire*, 1603

Pembrokeshire of 1603 when he illustrated the denuded chambered tomb of Pentre Ifan [4]. The Stonehenge drawings approximate to an axonometric projection seen from the west, but the castellated masonry over the far hill shows the artist drawing not what he saw, but what he heard, for there lies the Iron Age hill-fort of Ogbury, and such earthworks were commonly called 'Castle' by the Wessex peasantry up till yesterday. And here literature begins to affect the draughtsman's eye, the sway of conventions in verbal form. The learned world of early modern England was taking note of medieval legend; Geoffrey of Monmouth was first printed by Jerome Commelin at Heidelberg in 1587, and he and others had called Stonehenge *chorea gigantum*, the giants' dance, while Camden, the first edition of whose *Britannia* was published in 1586, had said that the monument [5] was 'such as Cicero termeth *Insanam substructionem*' (quoting from the *Pro Milone*). Dancing giants and a crazy structure became part of the 'requirement' of a Stonehenge view, and so R.F. and his followers, illustrating Camden himself, fantasticated the solid stones of a monument they had never seen. Smith's stones sternly resist the invitation to join the dance.

11

A. *Saxa quæ vocantur* Corfeftones *pondere.12.tonnar,*
   altitudine.24.pedes, latitudine pedes.7. ambitu.16.
B. *Saxa quæ vocantur* Cronett. *6.vel.7. tonnarum*
C. *Locus vbi ossa humana effodiuntur*

The topographers and antiquaries of the later seventeenth century brought Stonehenge down to earth again, from a whimsical projection to a sober eye-level view. John Aubrey, as is well known, made the first plan of the monument in 1666, a famous document of field arch-aeology, which appeared as Plate VII of his *Monumenta Britannica*, and I think most of us have taken his pen-and-wash view [6] in Plate VI to be an original sketch. There can be no doubt, unfortunately, that it is a copy not of nature but of Inigo Jones [7], an illustration to his book on Stonehenge, posthumously published by his kinsman John Webb in 1655 and demonstrating that it was a Roman temple. For the next original drawing we must turn to the superb views of David Loggan made somewhere in the last quarter of the seventeenth century [8]. These engravings, seen by young William Stukeley at the age of twenty-nine, first fired his enthusiasm for Stonehenge and his contempt for Camden's treatment of the monument – 'such a wretched anile account, as tis hard to say whether that or his draught of it be most false and trifling' – and so led to his own first-hand records, which go beyond topography and become the deliberate products of the field archaeologist.

The changing vision of Stonehenge has taken us from the fourteenth to the eighteenth century, and I want now to return to the end of the Middle Ages and the rediscovery of classical Antiquity on the one hand, and the new scientific approach on the other, represented in England by Francis Bacon at the beginning of the seventeenth century and culminating in the foundation of the Royal Society in its second half. In the Renaissance, students of Antiquity moved towards archaeology and its visual representation along two paths which frequently crossed or coalesced. In the first place, texts in manuscripts were inevitably linked to texts in inscriptions – monumental upon stone, in miniature on coins, gems and minor objects – and as accurate transcription was textually important, epigraphy went beyond transliteration as letter forms were seen to have value in themselves (in parallel to manuscript palaeography) and so inscriptions were drawn in at least approximate facsimile. The second path to the past was through architecture and works of art which might also carry inscriptions, so that here depiction and transcription coalesced, and artist and scholar met on common ground. Once the

6 JOHN AUBREY, Stonehenge, pen-and-wash, 1666, from his
unpublished *Monumenta Britannica*

7 INIGO JONES, Stonehenge, from *The Most Notable Antiquity of Great Britain vulgarly called Stone-Heng*, 1655

Sold by Henry Overton at

STONE-HENGE

ENGE *From the south*

8 DAVID LOGGAN, Stonehenge from the west and the south, *c.* 1675–1700

9 Ste Geneviève guarding her sheep, a sixteenth-century painting showing a now destroyed stone circle at Nanterre

classical canon of art and architecture became accepted, Vitruvius was read and illustrated, and 'drawing from the Antique' in the widest sense of the term was established.

Prehistoric antiquities could on occasion make an unexpected appearance in a work of art, as in the sixteenth-century painting of the patron saint of Paris, Ste Geneviève [9], guarding her sheep in a convincingly depicted stone circle, almost certainly a now destroyed monument at Nanterre.[3] But as an example of conscious antiquarian draughtsmanship of the early fifteenth century I select the work of Cyriac of Ancona,[4] not only for what Bernard Ashmole called the 'natural music' of his name, but because, as he went on to say in his study of Cyriac's drawings, 'as an archaeological observer he was at least a

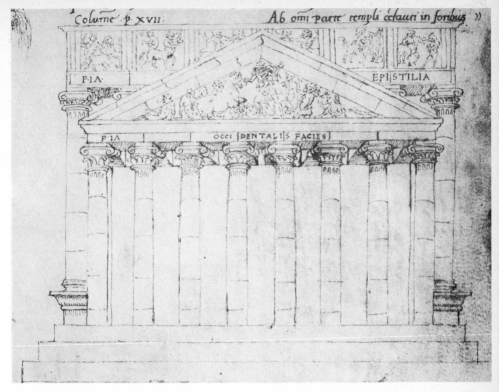

PIA·

EPISTILIA

PIA

OCCI DENTALIS FACIES

10 CYRIAC OF ANCONA, The Parthenon, 1436, copy by Giuliano da Sangallo; c. 1510

century ahead of his time' [10]. Born in 1391, he learnt Latin and Greek, held diplomatic appointments and travelled widely in Italy, Greece, the Aegean and even Egypt, was in Constantinople in the siege of 1453, and died a couple of years or so later. His drawings exist in five manuscripts in which the extreme complexity of originals and copies has been untangled in part by Ashmole: for our purpose the general nature of his record and style can be gathered from either, and the accuracy of his performance checked in more than one instance, both in epigraphy and in architectural detail. Ashmole has caught the copyists at their tricks – for instance turning the unfamiliar classical columns of a Greek temple into Gothic versions they understood – but enough of the originals have come through for us to applaud their sincerity.

19

11 PETER PAUL RUBENS' drawing, 1622, of the *Gemma Tiberiana*

12 The *Gemma Tiberiana*, Roman cameo in the Bibliothèque Nationale, Paris

Cyriac was also interested in coins and antique gems, which were of course to be increasingly admired, collected and illustrated. What would have been the earliest and most remarkable publication of classical gems and related carvings was never completed; though some of the drawings survive, by none other than Peter Paul Rubens [11], who was collaborating between 1621 and 1637 with the French scholar and antiquary Nicholas Claude Fabri de Pieresc in such a projected book.[5] Peiresc had discovered a huge first-century cameo, the *Gemma Tiberiana* [12], set in a fourteenth-century reliquary in the treasury of Ste-Chapelle in Paris, while Rubens had recently drawn another, the *Gemma Augustea*, in the Imperial Cabinet in Vienna. Both intended to publish and agreed to collaborate, but on Peiresc's death in 1637 the work, which had involved an international team of scholars and assembled nineteen drawings of gems by Rubens, never appeared, though drawings and engravings survive. This precocious plan for a corpus antedates the *Thesauri* of Graevius and Gronovius, published 1694–1702, the *Antiquité expliquée* of Bernard de Montfaucon (1719) and the *Recueil d'antiquités* of the Comte de Caylus in seven volumes published 1752–67, at a time when the antiquaries were being derided by the French *philosophes*. We think better of them today, and respect Montfaucon for firmly stating that for him Antiquity was 'what can be seen, and what can be represented in illustration', and Caylus for illustrating not only works of art but such things as Samian sherds [13].[6]

But we must retrace our steps and explore other pathways to the past, those of the early scientists, who were to take up their positions in the Battle of the Ancients and the Moderns in the seventeenth century,[7] and in so doing were to explore a new model of visual representation, a new 'requirement' in Sir Ernst's phrase. The debate, as is well known, centred on the question of the Ancients as exemplars: had civilization reached its summit in classical Antiquity, to be followed by a melan-choly decline down to and including the Moderns, or could it be that the modern world of the seventeenth century had made advances at least in science and technology; was the last word to be with Aristotle or with Bacon? What is of interest to us here is that even the champions of what became the Royal Society approach, such as Joseph Glanvill, did 'not believe the moderns surpass the ancients in Architecture, Picture, or the Arts of ingenuous Luxury', thereby removing the study of classical art and archaeology from the new learning. But illustration was important to the scientists to an increasing degree as they turned from ancient literary authority to a first-hand empirical study of phenomena, and in England especially we can see how non-classical archaeology, antiquities which were not works of art, became the province of the early fellowship of the Royal Society. They were included under two categories, as portable antiquities such as prehistoric stone or bronze tools, or pottery, on the one hand, and as field monuments ranging from prehistoric to medieval on the other: within the prevailing canons of aesthetic criticism, the Middle Ages were barbarian, and could not therefore contain acceptable architecture or works of art.

Pl. CV

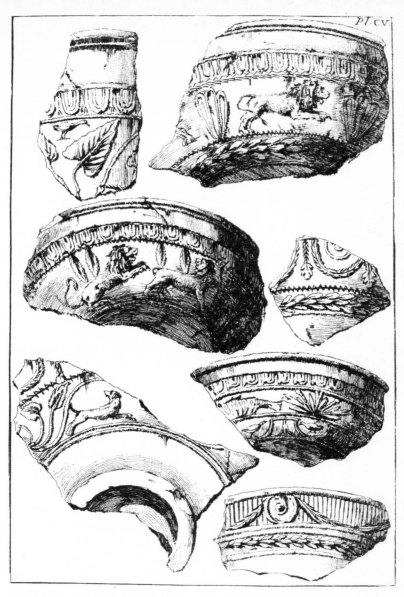

13 Samian sherds, from the Comte de Caylus' *Recueil d'antiquités*, 1752–67

I recently suggested[8] that from the Renaissance, on the Continent and in Britain, we could recognize two types of collections of antiquities being made, cherished and displayed. In the first place come the descendants of the medieval church or cathedral treasury, the *Kunstkammer* or secular and patrician, if not royal, collection of works of art in which classical sculpture rapidly predominated, and I instanced as an English example the Arundel Marbles, assembled by Thomas Howard, second Earl of Arundel from 1625, the remains of which, after extraordinary vicissitudes, came to Oxford in 1667; as a later example we might topically add the classical sculpture collected by Charles Townley from 1768 onwards, and now about to be exhumed from the cellars of the British Museum. For such collections catalogues with illustrations were of course prepared or, as we saw with Peiresc and Rubens, scholars could assemble works of art from diverse sources for depiction. But the second type of Renaissance museum, taken up and developed in seventeenth-century England, was what I characterized as 'scientific and mercantile', and as such very much a part of the assembling of first-hand knowledge with which the early Royal Society was consciously and devotedly concerned. Stukeley after all at the beginning of the next century spoke of 'the Study of Antiquities or any other Science'.

These Cabinets of Curiosities might sometimes contain works of art such as coins, more suited than marbles to the modest purse, but by the end of the seventeenth century some, like Archbishop Wake who bequeathed his coin cabinet to Christ Church, Oxford, saw coins as historical documents and their value as didactic. But in the main the collections were associated with natural history, and especially botany, and the formation not only of herbaria, but of 'physic gardens' and gardens for pleasure 'containing the new exotic plants becoming available for medicine, industry, the kitchen and personal delight as trade developed with the Orient, and increasingly with the Americas'.[9] The importance of illustration in the early explorations of foreign lands was recognized from the first: that enchanting artist John White [14], who accompanied Sir Richard Grenville and Sir Walter Raleigh to Virginia between 1585 and 1590, recorded the natural history as well as

14 JOHN WHITE, An Indian village in Virginia, watercolour, *c.*1585–90

the ethnography of the new land, and the similar records made two centuries later in the Pacific under Cook, Bankes and others are well known.[10] The Royal Society from its beginnings sought to have information recorded in 'Plotts and Draughts' by 'Seamen, bound for far voyages, that they may increase their Philosophical Stock', and when ethnographic objects were brought home, and made a part of the Society's Museum of Natural and Artificial Rarities, of the Tradescants' Ark, of the museums of Sir Thomas Browne or Ralph Thoresby or Sir Robert Sibbald in this country, or of Ole Worm in Copenhagen, they also needed illustration.

25

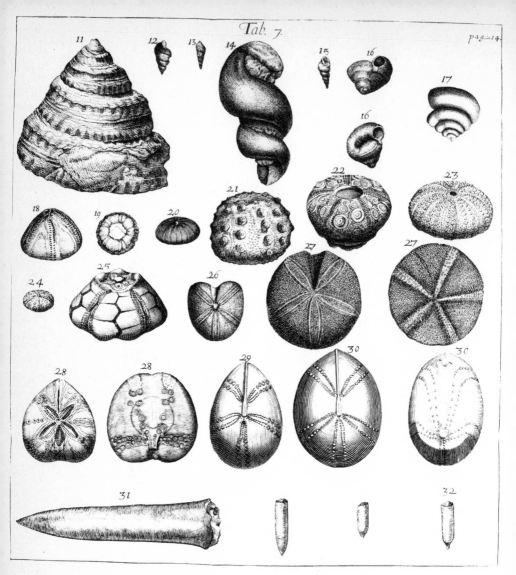

15 MARTIN LISTER, *Fossils*, from *Historia animalium angliae*, 1678

26

Plants in particular needed depiction, as the beginnings of taxonomic botany emerged with for instance John Ray; and visual identification of medicinal plants was obviously necessary if the patient was not to be dosed with belladonna rather than elecampane by an incompetent herbalist relying only on verbal descriptions. Botanical illustration consequently early acquired a competence and accuracy in response to a very real and practical 'requirement' by professional men, and with the growing needs of taxonomy in other fields of natural history other categories of living things were being illustrated. Martin Lister published an *Historia animalium* in 1678 with illustrations of fossils [15], and between 1685 and 1691 his great work on molluscan shells, *Historia sive synopsis methodica conchyliorum*, with over a thousand engravings of all shells then known: a family affair, as the drawings were by his wife and his two daughters Susannah and Mary. To practical needs we may add human and animal anatomy, and anatomical collections and their illustration, a vast field we cannot explore here, though it is interesting that the great antiquarian draughtsman William Stukeley was a doctor of medicine who published anatomical drawings of an elephant and of the human spleen. But while the museums and their catalogues were normally severely scientific in concept and display, eccentricity was always lurking, as it was with antiquarianism, and the anatomical museum of Frederik Ruysch at Amsterdam [16], as we know it from its catalogue of 1704, was eccentric to the point of surrealism.

Against this background of increasingly accurate delineation of natural history we turn to antiquities. To the seventeenth century, stone antiquities – flint arrowheads, stone axe-heads or battle-axes – were inseparably associated with what we would now distinguish as crystals, minerals and fossils, as 'formed stones'. As such, they formed part of the scientific collections and the illustrations of them, and though their association there with ethnographical specimens of stone tools led the more perceptive scholars to identify them for what they were, prehistoric artifacts, acceptance was by no means immediate. The history of their recognition went side by side with that of fossils as extinct organisms; bilaterally symmetrical, they were catalogued among 'regular formed stones'. Mercati's precocious identifications of the late sixteenth century

16 Plate from the catalogue of Frederik Ruysch's anatomical museum, Amsterdam, 1744

17 Prehistoric implements, figurine, and Early Christian crosses,
from Robert Plot's *Natural History of Staffordshire*, 1686 ▷

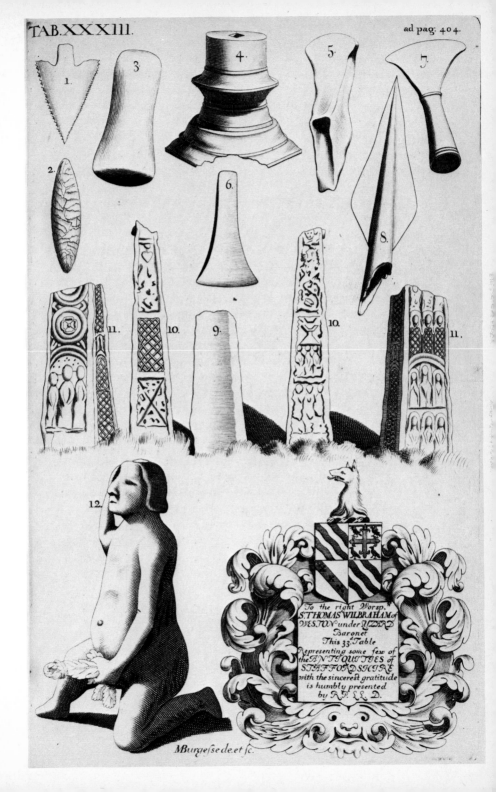

TAB.XXXIII.

ad pag: 404.

1. 2. 3. 4. 5. 6. 7. 8. 9. 10. 11. 12.

To the right Worsp.
S.ʳ THOMAS WILBRAHAM of
WESTON under UZEAD
Baronet
This 33.ᵗ Table
Representing some few of
the ANTIQUITIES of
STAFFORDSHIRE
with the sincerest gratitude
is humbly presented
by R.ᵗ P. LL.D.

M. Burgesse de. et sc.

18 CHARLES
RENNIE
MACKINTOSH,
Larkspur, 1914

were not published until 1717. Meanwhile Dugdale in 1656 had said that some Warwickshire stone axes were 'weapons used by Britons before the art of making arms of brass or iron was known', and in 1686 Robert Plot was also accepting that ancient Britons 'for the most part at least . . . sharpen'd their *warlike instruments* rather with *stones* than *metall*' [17], and illustrating them among antiquities and not fossils, together with Bronze Age tools and the late Saxon cross-shafts at Checkley in Staffordshire. The illustrations are by Michael Burghers, the Dutchman who became engraver to the University of Oxford and also illustrated Plot's *Oxfordshire*, fossils for Edward Lhwyd, and the Stonesfield Roman pavement for Thomas Hearne.

30

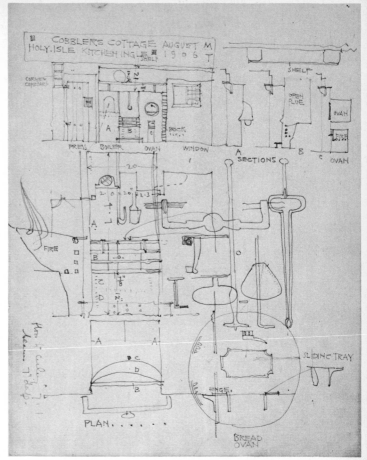

In the publications of the early topographers, of whom Plot was one, the same draughtsman would illustrate plants, animals, fossils, coins, antiquities and buildings. Sir Robert Sibbald employed Robert Miln and George Main as illustrators; Aubrey, and rather later Stukeley, did their own drawings. Sensitive draughtsmanship could make itself felt in more than one direction, and to jump the centuries we might compare the flower drawings [18] with the architectural details [19] of Charles Rennie Macintosh. With the early drawings of prehistoric objects, as with the illustrations of fossils, accuracy and faithful delineation increased partly in response to the needs of scholars and partly as the nature of the object was less imperfectly understood, the fossil being seen

31

as an organism and the flint arrowhead as a humanly flaked artifact. Yet even without archaeological recognition, accurate enough information can be conveyed by adequate draughtsmanship: although Sir Thomas Browne in 1658, and Sir Robert Sibbald in 1710, published cinerary urns both believed to be Roman, their illustrations show us convincingly the pagan Saxon pots which were their originals [20, 21]. In the later Saxon field, George Hickes, the great Anglo-Saxon scholar, published in 1704 a drawing of an eleventh-century silver disc brooch from the Isle of Ely which then vanished from sight until it was brought into the British Museum in 1950 and immediately identified from what could then be recognized as a highly accurate drawing [22]. Coins, and numismatic draughtsmanship, deserve extended and specialist treatment on their own, and here we can do no more than remind ourselves of the long and honourable tradition of illustrating the prehistoric British coinage, going back to the very beginning of the seventeenth century with Speed and Camden.

I said that two categories of antiquities presented themselves to the antiquaries of the seventeenth century, portable objects and field monuments. We must now turn to the latter, and here, of course, going back to the Gombrich quotation with which we began, we must consider the 'purpose and requirements of the society in which the given visual language gains currency'. The new antiquarianism was intimately bound up with the new topographical approach to the British countryside, and the countryside was becoming the subject of the landscape artist. Local antiquities were to take their place in the new depiction of landscape, just as classical buildings formed a component in the admired archetypes of the painters, the canvases of Claude or Poussin; a growing pride in the home product, fostered by the Moderns as against the Ancients, encouraged the depiction of local architecture and ruins. The way was pointed by immigrants bringing pictorial traditions from Europe. Wenceslaus Hollar was brought to England from Bohemia in 1635 by no less than the second Earl of Arundel, whose sculpture collection we have already noted; David Loggan was a Danziger, in England before 1653, engraver successively to the Universities of Oxford and Cambridge (we have seen his Stonehenge

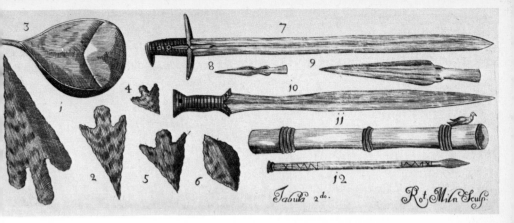

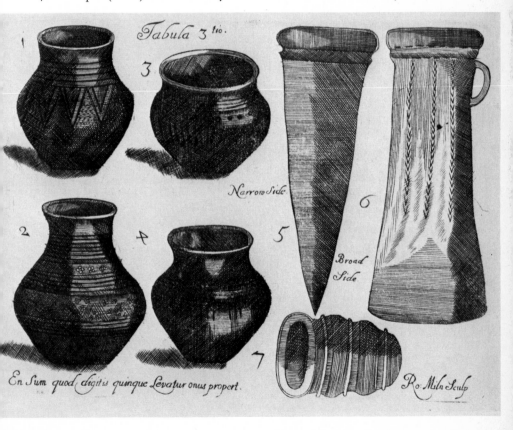

20, 21 Illustrations from Sir Robert Sibbald's *Miscellanea quaedam eruditae antiquitatis*, 1710. The pots (below) were believed by him to be Roman but were evidently Saxon

drawings); Michael Burghers, another name we have met, came from Amsterdam to Oxford in 1673, where he succeeded Loggan as University Engraver. Connections with the antiquaries was inevitable. Hollar was a friend of John Aubrey, who described him as 'a very friendly good-natured man as could be'. He engraved a drawing of Aubrey's for the *Monasticon*, and among an enormous output of work illustrated the original catalogue of the Tradescant Museum of 1656. He was also a friend of Francis Place, who will concern us in a moment, and helped and encouraged him in etching and print-making. Loggan at least indirectly inspired Stukeley; Burghers, as we saw, was a friend of Plot, Lhwyd and Hearne. Michael van der Gucht was an Antwerp engraver who came to London in 1690, and his son Gerard was a friend of William Stukeley and the best engraver of his drawings.

Francis Place,[11] born in 1647, was a Yorkshire gentleman who, said Vertue, 'passed his time at ease, being a sociable & pleasant companion much belov'd by the Gentry' [23]. But it was no idle ease, for he was to become by the end of the century a distinguished English landscape artist in line, wash and watercolour. In earlier life a friend of Hollar, he had characteristically also illustrated for Martin Lister, and drawn and engraved insects and shells for Godaert's *Of Insects* in 1682–5. He showed the contemporary interest in the practical application of science by setting up a potters' kiln producing an individual style of salt-glazed stoneware; as a member of the group of York Virtuosi he was also much in contact with the antiquaries, drawing medieval buildings for Ralph Thoresby's *Ducatus Leodinensis*, published in 1715, and for Francis Drake's *Eboracum*, finally published seven years after his death, in 1729. In Place we have the beginning of the combined topographical and antiquarian draughtsmanship which continued through such artists as the brothers Buck and the brothers Sandby, and which, encouraged by new methods of reproduction such as aquatint (and eventually lithography), was such a feature of the antiquarian and topographical journalism made popular by, and itself popularizing, the Romantic Movement and the Picturesque Tour from the later decades of the eighteenth century.

22 Above: Drawing by GEORGE HICKES of an eleventh-century silver disc brooch from the Isle of Ely, 1704. Below: photograph of the actual brooch, rediscovered in 1950

23 Francis
Place, York
Minster, c.1710

To return to the relationship between accuracy of representation and the degree of understanding of the nature of the subject depicted, Sir Ernst has made some illuminating comments on architectural detail in topographical draughtsmanship. He instances Matthäus Merian's apparently accurate view of Nôtre-Dame in Paris, of about 1635, in which, however, 'as a child of the seventeenth century, his notion of a church is that of a lofty symmetrical building with large, rounded windows' and he re-designs Nôtre-Dame accordingly. Even a couple of centuries later, in 1836, an English artist, all too elevated by the aesthetic and moral beauties of the Pointed Style, could impose it upon the Romanesque structure of the west front of Chartres.[12] In England in the seventeenth century and most of the eighteenth, the difficulty behind delineation of Gothic architecture, was as with fossils or arrowheads, not an incapacity to draw accurately but a failure to understand the subject matter. The slow progress in the recognition that the buildings of the Middle Ages were not only self-consciously architectural concepts, often of considerable subtlety, but that they exhibited an internal stylistic development from pre-Conquest to Perpendicular, is well known. A radical conceptual re-adjustment had to be made, in the creation of a new canon of taste for those who even if they were Moderns, still held, as we saw Glanvill did, that they 'did not surpass the ancients in Architecture', and that the Middle Ages were a lamentable Gothic and barbarian morass from which, with Vitruvius in one hand and Palladio in the other, contemporary architects were struggling to emerge. John Aubrey was a pioneer in devising an architectural taxonomy in parallel with those of the natural sciences, by a close observation of detail tied to examples dated from documentary sources: when he wrote 'the windows ye most remarqueable, hence one may give a guess about what Time the Building was', he was depending on an accurate observation of form and structure in window-head and tracery, and his rough sketches bear this out [24]. But his *Chronologia Architectonica* of the 1670s was unpublished and bore no fruit, and Thomas Warton's scheme of 1762, the first published attempt at chronological ordering, was brief, unillustrated, quirky in nomenclature (Saxon, Gothic Saxon, Absolute Gothic) and buried in a commentary on Spenser's *Faerie Queene*. A lack

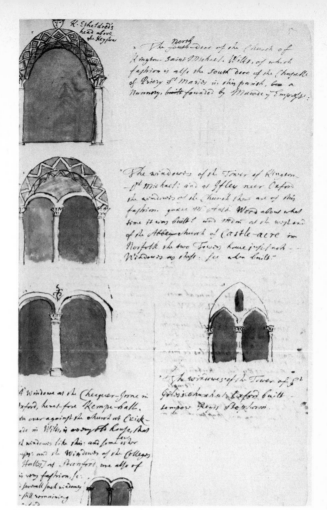

of understanding of the underlying geometry of the tracery of the west window of York Minster, for instance, can be seen in Place's view of about 1710, quite apart from inaccuracies in other respects, such as the surrounding stone panelling. But we must not be unfair to Place, nor to Hollar, Burghers and the rest of the topograhical draughtsmen of the time, in judging them by standards not those of their age, and which indeed they might have found difficult of comprehension. So far as contemporary 'requirement' went, they met it, and sometimes exceeded its modest needs.

39

For architecture, formal models of representation in plan, section, elevation and perspective had long been available and, once the styles were appreciated and increasingly understood, were easily applicable to Gothic or to the tiny fragments of Roman architecture still remaining above ground in Britain. With prehistoric or early historic field monuments there were no precedents in representation, and the 'requirement' for their visual record had to be conceived *de novo* before it could act as norm: what did one antiquary in the field wish to convey to another? I have suggested[13] that the recognition of ancient earthwork defences may have been easier to generations to whom Renaissance fortification was a living tradition, recently deployed in the Civil War, than to more modern times. The most obvious need was for plans, and here there was no need to seek the fortress architect or professional surveyor when surveying was a country gentleman's accomplishment taught in the seventeenth-century Inns of Court: as early as 1621 the author of *The Anatomy of Melancholy* found land-surveying and map-making a pleasurable antidote. Even if the vague and amorphous outlines of long-denuded, grass-grown banks and ditches might cause problems of representation – as indeed they do to field archaeologists today – accuracy in the ground-plan was not hard to attain if the need for that accuracy was felt among scholars. Of course it was not, any more than in the eighteenth or nineteenth century before the advent of modern archaeology in the person of General Pitt-Rivers and such as followed him. Aubrey tells us he used a plane-table for his famous Avebury survey [25], 'projected by the halfe inch scale' of half an inch to one chain of twenty-two yards: in the early 1620s, Edmund Gunter, professor of astronomy at Gresham College, had introduced the chain for land surveying that still bears his name. The resultant plan in the *Monumenta* is a sketched approximation to this scale, in which Aubrey exaggerates the departure from a circular plan of the bank and ditch, with an undue emphasis on its nearly straight segments, but this does not detract from the achievement of planning a twenty-eight-acre site divided by field hedges and containing at least some houses. William Stukeley's plan of 1724 [26] in its published form also seems to have been intended to be at about this scale, but here the main fault is the

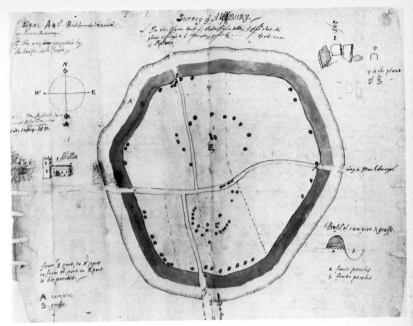

25 JOHN AUBREY,
Survey of Avebury,
from his
unpublished
*Monumenta
Britannica*, c.1675

26 WILLIAM
STUKELEY,
'Groundplot' of
Avebury, 1724.
From his
Abury, 1743.

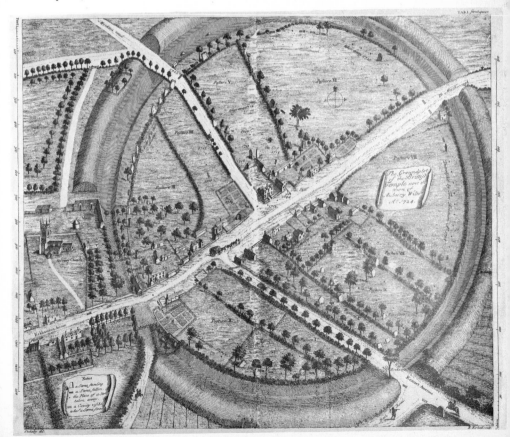

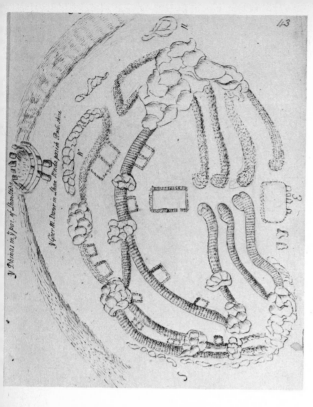

27 WILLIAM JONES,
Plan of Y Garn
Fawr, Llanwnda,
Pembrokeshire, made
for Edward Lhwyd,
1697–8

28 Modern survey of ▷
the same hill-fort

assumption that the monument is a geometrically compass-drawn circle, giving a contrary series of errors, though with greatly increased detail of the stones and of the encumbrances to survey offered by village and hedgerows. But all in all, the two plans between them form most remarkable records, a couple of generations apart, of the monument, and are a tribute to the competence of two amateur draughtsmen and nascent archaeologists in the very dawn of the subject.

On the whole, prehistoric hill-forts and earthworks were not made the objects of visual record by the antiquaries of the seventeenth and early eighteenth centuries, though Roman forts and camps in north Britain were being planned, with varying degrees of accuracy, by such as Alexander Gordon in his *Itinerarium Septentrionale* of 1726. It was widely held that Iron Age hill-forts were Roman too, but Edward Lhwyd recognized the Welsh forts for what they were and had plans made by one of his young assistants, William Jones, in 1697–8 [27]. It seems

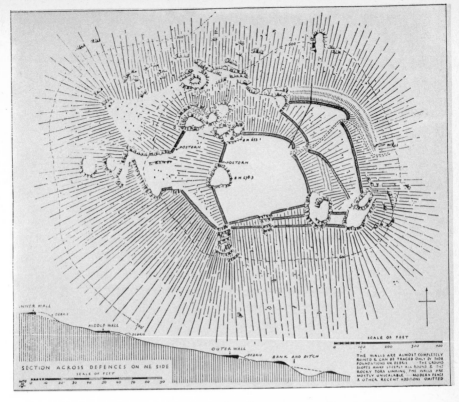

INNER WALL

MIDDLE WALL

DEBRIS

OUTER WALL

SECTION ACROSS DEFENCES ON NE SIDE
SCALE OF FEET

DEBRIS

BANK AND DITCH

SCALE OF FEET

THE WALLS ARE ALMOST COMPLETELY
RUINED & CAN BE TRACED ONLY BY THEIR
FOUNDATIONS OR DEBRIS THE GROUND
SLOPES AWAY STEEPLY ALL ROUND & THE
ROCKY TORS LINKING THE WALLS ARE
MOSTLY UNSCALABLE · MODERN FENCE
& OTHER RECENT ADDITIONS OMITTED

hardly fair to this piece of pioneer fieldwork to compare the plan of Y Garn Fawr at Llanwnda in Pembrokeshire (Dyfed) with a modern survey [28], and find it grotesquely inaccurate, and anyone who has planned ancient monuments on Welsh mountain-tops will have every sympathy with poor Jones. He also, and more successfully, made the earliest plan of the famous Irish neolithic passage-grave of New Grange in 1699. This was soon followed by another published in 1726 by Sir Thomas Molyneux in Dublin, together with some quite recognizable Bronze Age pots: Molyneux was a physician and a leading spirit in the Dublin Philosophical Society of 1683–1708. In Wales at this time Henry Rowlands published his *Mona Antiqua Illustrata* with his own drawings of Anglesey megaliths and other antiquities: they are weirdly incompetent but at least an attempt at visual presentation. Stukeley published his fully illustrated *Itinerarium Curiosum* in 1724 and his Stonehenge and Avebury volumes in 1740–3 with his drawings of

43

twenty years earlier. The early eighteenth century carried on the Royal Society tradition of archaeology that began with Aubrey and Plot: science-based, empirical and factual, in parallel with natural history and palaeontology, and demanding appropriate illustration. Robert Hooke saw as complementary the antiquary who studied human artifacts and the 'Natural Antiquary' who studied fossils.

It was a propitious beginning, but by the 1730s, as is well known, changing moods were bringing about a decline in the standards of many disciplines, including the natural sciences, historical research and the tentative emergence of archaeology: 'The mood was shifting from rational to romantic, from classical calm to barbarian excitement. Though British antiquities were now to become popular, and a part of the country's intellectual and artistic life as never before, they were being seen through very different eyes from those of Aubrey or the young Stukeley'.[14] We enter a phase when ancient monuments are seen in terms of the Picturesque: William Gilpin was disappointed by Stonehenge when he visited it, describing it as 'totally void, though in a ruinous state, of every idea of picturesque beauty . . . the stones are so uncouthly placed, that we found it impossible to form them, from any stand, into a pleasing shape'.[15] This was in 1798, the heyday of the Tours in Search of the Picturesque and the illustrated books they engendered – Thomas Pennant with his Tours in Wales and Scotland in 1771–8, Francis Grose's *Antiquities* of England, Wales and Scotland from 1773 to 1791, and all the others, leading into the next century with Britton and Brayley's *Beauties* and *Architectural Beauties* of Britain between 1801 and 1814. Architecture and natural beauty, antiquities and the Picturesque, were still one in the minds of many; for the antiquarian revival we have to wait for such major publications as Sir Richard Colt Hoare's *Ancient History of Wiltshire* in five parts between 1810 and 1821 (a prelude to his *Modern History* of 1822–44, which begins with Domesday Book). Its novelty and significance lies less in the quality of the illustrations occupying seventy-seven folio engraved plates, than that it was in fact a prehistoric and Roman archaeology of the county, based on first-hand fieldwork and excavation. This was planned and directed by Hoare and carried out by William

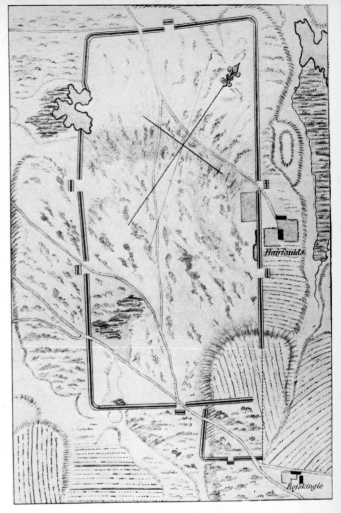

Within the image: *Hairkuild*, *Rofskingie*

29 WILLIAM ROY,
Plan of Roman
camp near
Kirkboddo, from
*The Military
Antiquities of the
Romans in North
Britain*, 1773

Cunnington, with the illustrations made by Hoare's own draughtsman Philip Crocker, originally a surveyor and draughtsman in the newly formed Ordnance Survey but in Hoare's employment on the Stourhead estate from 1811. The Survey's first Director General was William Roy, who began his career in Scotland in 1747–55 on a mapping project in which he employed Paul Sandby, so linking the artist to the map. In 1773 Roy completed his great study of Roman field monuments, *The Military Antiquities of the Romans in North Britain*, with its fine plans of forts and camps [29]. Roman antiquities had been well served earlier in

45

30, 31 Roman carved slab from Bridgeness, marking the eastern end of the
Antonine Wall (above), and (below) an engraving of the same published by JOHN
HORSLEY in *Britannia Romana*, 1732

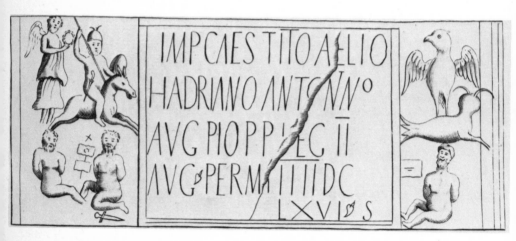

the eighteenth century by John Horsley's *Britannia Romana* of 1732, but it
is interesting to notice that although he could accurately transcribe
inscriptions and make judicious historical use of them, his vision could
not accommodate Romano-British sculpture, which appears in his
plates in woeful travesty [30, 31]. Roman mosaic pavements, in a
classical idiom that could be comprehended, were often extremely well
portrayed, as for instance by Michael Burghers at Stonesfield in 1712 or
by George Vertue at Littlecote in 1730 [32].

46

32 GEORGE VERTUE, Roman pavement found at Littlecote, Wiltshire, 1730 ▷

33 'MR GUEST' OF SALISBURY, Beaker and grave goods in a landscape at
Winterslow, oil painting, 1814

There are some charming instances of excavated antiquities forming a
part of a pictorial composition, as in the beaker and its associated grave
goods set in their own landscape at Winterslow in Mr Guest of
Salisbury's painting of 1814 [33]. In the mode of the moment too was
the trompe l'œil presentation of antiquities as if on loose sheets of paper,
like the Siberian finds of Cornelius Witsen of Amsterdam in 1785 [34],
or the Anglo-Saxon antiquities of James Douglas in 1793 [35], of
which more later. Not only Stonehenge, but other megalithic
monuments, could now form subjects for Romantic paintings, and

48

34 CORNELIUS WITSEN, Jewellery from Siberia,
from *Noord en Oost Tartarye*, 1785 ▷

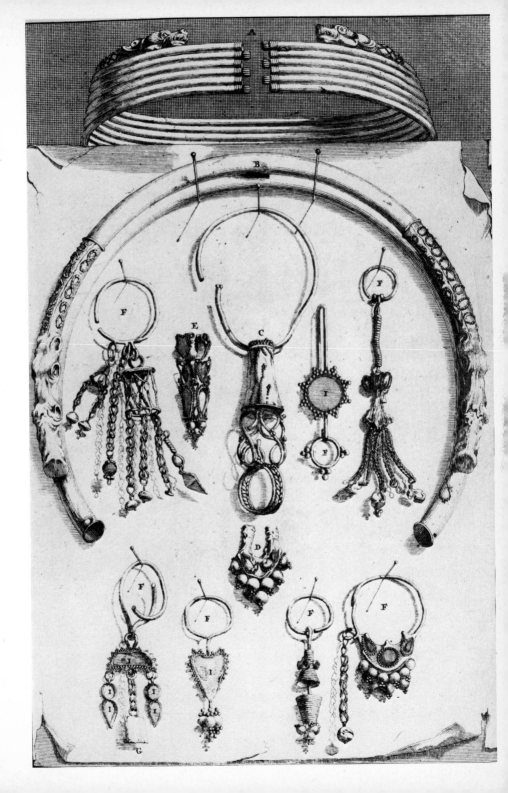

35 JAMES DOUGLAS,
Anglo-Saxon
antiquities, from *Nenia
Britannica*, 1793

Richard Tonge of Bath described himself as 'painter and modeller of Megaliths' around 1830 when he painted the Pentre Ifan chambered tomb in Pembrokeshire [36]. This new megalithic vision could be transferred to antiquities in distant lands, as William Hodges' splendid painting of the Easter Island statues [37], from drawings made in 1774 on Cook's second voyage, shows us.[16] Hodges, a pupil of Richard Wilson, had exhibited in 1768 a painting at the Society of Artists called *A View of a Druids' Altar in Pembrokeshire*, which surely must have been of Pentre Ifan too, and his Easter Island painting has strange affinities with Tonge's later view of Pentre Ifan: the skull at the foot of the pillars must, as Bernard Smith saw, echo the *Et in Arcadia ego* theme, but is nearer to the Guercino and earlier Poussin versions than to the later where, as with Richard Wilson's own treatment, the skull is absent.

36 RICHARD TONGUE, Chamber tomb of Pentre Ifan, Pembrokeshire, oil-painting, 1830

37 WILLIAM HODGES, Statues on Easter Island, oil-painting, after 1774

The pioneer in Britain of the systematic illustration of a large series of excavated antiquities was James Douglas,[17] Captain of Ordnance Engineers at Chatham as a young man and ordained in 1783 – 'a man of most varied talents' as a member of Peterhouse, his Cambridge college, was to describe him. He illustrated and described the contents of Anglo-Saxon graves excavated by himself in Kent, and appears to have been the first to recognize pagan Saxon antiquities for what they were. An able artist, he drew and engraved his own plates, published from 1786 in parts as *Nenia Britannica*, British Funeral Dirges, an odd title for which however he obtained Samuel Johnson's approval. 'The engravings are finished in *Aqua Tinta*', he wrote in his prospectus. 'This style of Engraving is happily adapted to the nature of Antique Relics, as it conveys a correct Idea of the Originals' – though as we saw he sometimes engaged in trompe l'œil whimsies. Aquatint had been introduced into England by Paul Sandby about 1750: a link through the Board of Ordnance and General Roy between topographical and archaeological draughtsmanship. Colt Hoare, who knew Douglas and admired his work, followed his example in the lay-out and illustration of antiquities in his *Ancient History of Wiltshire*.

By now we are moving into the last phase, when antiquarianism is becoming archaeology, and the 'requirements of the society in which the given visual language gains currency' are recognizably our own. The field is vast, and a few names only must suffice to span the nineteenth century and take us into the twentieth. Wood engraving and lithography became the favoured media, and with Orlando Jewitt, working from the early 1840s to the late 1860s, we have an illustrator in the old tradition, equally at home with his wood blocks for Bentham and Hooker's famous *Flora*, or with the enthusiasts of the Gothic Revival from Pugin to Parker and Bloxham, and the illustrations for *The Archaeological Journal*. A recent perceptive student of Jewitt's work wrote of his lithography that it was a medium in which 'he never did himself justice',[18] but here an archaeologist must register a protest, for his litho plates for the *Horae Ferales* of J. M. Kemble and A. W. Franks of 1863 'include some of the finest and most sympathetic renderings still available' of the masterpieces of British Early Celtic art and are a

38 ORLANDO JEWITT, British Early Celtic shield-bosses,
from J. M. Kemble and A. W. Franks. *Horae Ferales*, 1863

landmark in its appreciation [38]. Less than twenty years later,
completely modern archaeological publication and illustration leapt
fully armed into the Victorian scene in the form of the four great volumes
of General Pitt-Rivers' excavation reports of 1880–94. Pitt-Rivers, it is
surprising to realize, was a boy of eleven when Sir Richard Colt Hoare

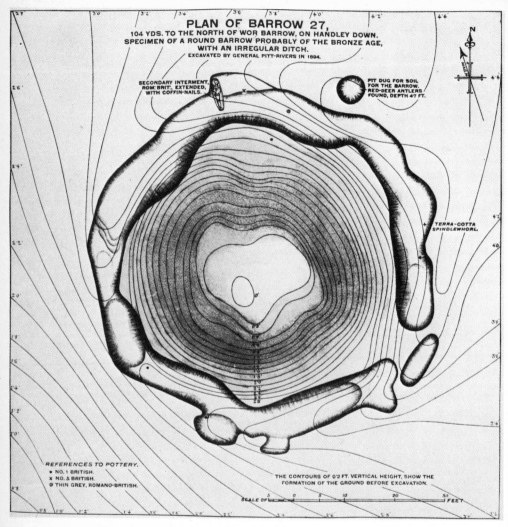

SECONDARY INTERMENT,
ROM: BRIT., EXTENDED,
WITH COFFIN-NAILS.

PIT DUG FOR SOIL
FOR THE BARROW.
RED-DEER ANTLERS
FOUND, DEPTH 4'7 FT.

TERRA-COTTA
SPINDLEWHORL.

REFERENCES TO POTTERY.
● NO. 1 BRITISH.
X NO. 3 BRITISH.
⊘ THIN GREY, ROMANO-BRITISH.

THE CONTOURS OF 0·2 FT. VERTICAL HEIGHT, SHOW THE
FORMATION OF THE GROUND BEFORE EXCAVATION.

SCALE OF   5   0   5   10   20   30   FEET

39 Plan of a round barrow on Handley Down, Cranborne Chase, from A. H. L.
Pitt-Rivers' *Excavations in Cranborne Chase*, 1887

died, and *he* had been born six years before William Stukeley's death: the three men spanned two formative centuries in the history of British field archaeology. Text was subordinate to illustration for the General, and the drawings are recognizably statements in a new visual language, his own [39]. They have, as I have said, 'a terse efficient style, calling to mind the gunner's world of arcs and sectors, field sketching and bushy-topped trees, and the publications of Messrs Gale and Polden of Aldershot'.[19]

Two more archaeological draughtsmen bring my superficial sketch down to our own day. The first linked field archaeology to a world of artistic conventions we glimpsed in Charles Rennie Macintosh: the tail end of Pre-Raphaelitism, the Art Workers' Guild, William Morris and C. F. Voysey. Heywood Sumner, born in 1853, was an artist in this tradition who had illustrated books and designed posters, wall-paper and stained glass, and who in 1904 settled at Gorley in the New Forest. Here he turned his talent to the record of the local earthworks, publishing with the Chiswick Press those of Cranborne Chase in 1913 and of the New Forest in 1917 [40, 42]. Unique and unrepeatable in style, they have an immense period charm, with a quality that just 'trod the tightrope between apt decoration and arty-crafty awfulness', but were not the real answer to the archaeologist's 'requirement' of the twentieth century. It was left for young Mortimer Wheeler in the 1920s and 1930s to make the last archaeological statement in draughtsmanship before elegance became suspect and outmoded, and diagrammatic austerity and the ineptitudes of misused Letraset took its place [41]. To the precision of Pitt-Rivers, Wheeler added his own restrained artistry, not least in lettering, and a sense of style and balance, which will remain a landmark in the long vista of those who strove, like Stukeley, 'to illustrate the monuments'.

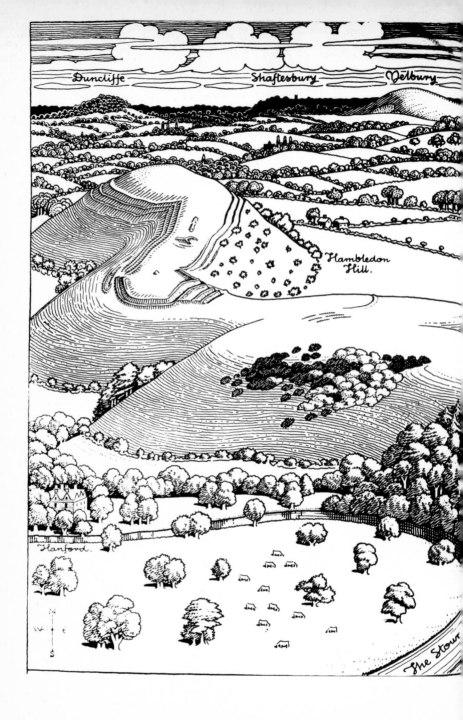

THE ANCIENT EARTHWORKS
OF CRANBORNE CHASE

Described, & Delineated in plans founded
on the 25 inch to 1 mile Ordnance Survey

by

Heywood Sumner. F.S.A.

With a Map shewing the physical features
& the ancient sites of Cranborne Chase
founded on the 1 inch to 1 mile Ordnance
Survey & coloured by hand ⁓ A.D. 1913

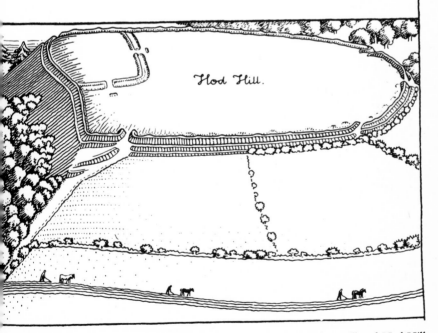

40 HEYWOOD SUMNER, Bird's-eye view of camps on Hambledon Hill and Hod Hill,
Cranborne Chase, 1913

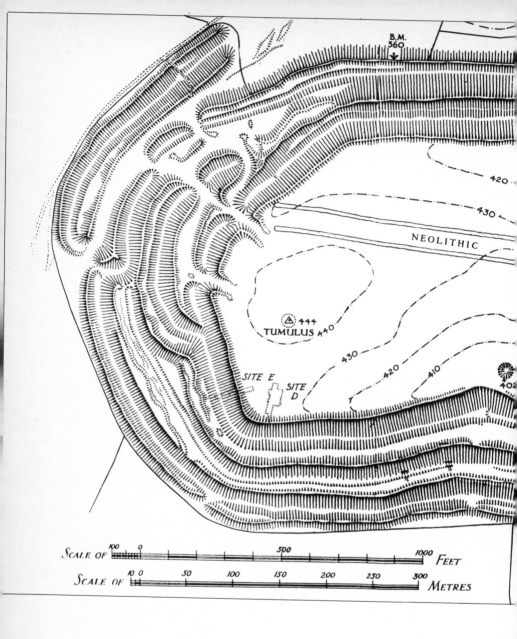

B.M.
360

420

430

NEOLITHIC

△ 444
TUMULUS 440

430

420

410

402

SITE E

SITE
D

SCALE OF   100 0   500   1000 FEET

SCALE OF   10 0   50   100   150   200   250   300 METRES

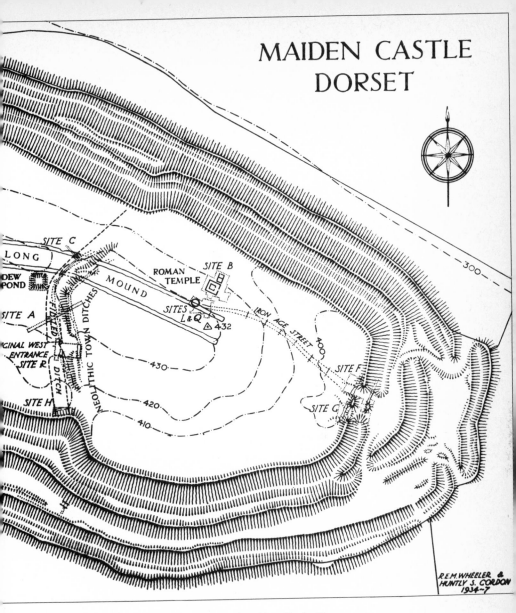

MAIDEN CASTLE
DORSET

SITE C

LONG

DEW
POND

ROMAN
TEMPLE

SITE B

SITE A

M O U N D

SITES
L & Q

△ 432

IRON AGE STREET

NEOLITHIC TOWN DITCHES

SILTED DITCH

SITE F

GINAL WEST
ENTRANCE
SITE R

430

400

SITE H

420

SITE G

410

300

R.E.M. WHEELER &
HUNTLY S. GORDON
1934-7

41 MORTIMER WHEELER, Plan of Maiden Castle, Dorset, 1934–7

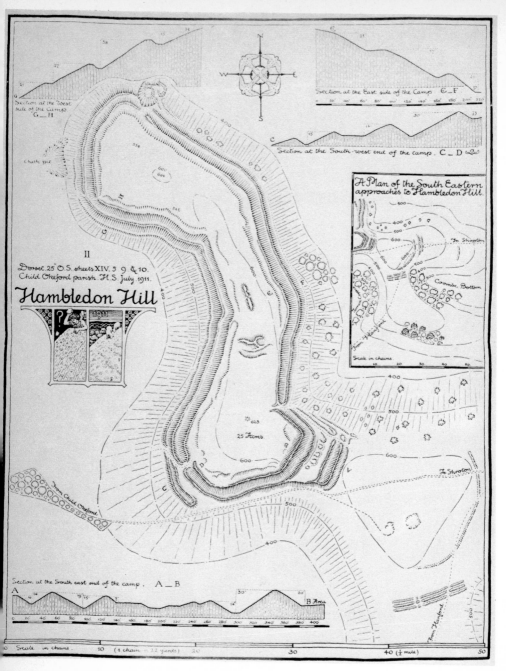

42 HEYWOOD SUMNER, Plan of Hambledon Hill, 1911

NOTES

LIST OF ILLUSTRATIONS

NOTES

1 General documentation in Stuart Piggott, *Ruins in a Landscape*, Edinburgh 1976, and *Antiq.* XXXIX, 1965, p. 165–76.
2 E. H. Gombrich, *Art and Illusion*, New York 1960, p. 90.
3 *Antiq.* XLVII, 1973, p. 292; XLVIII, 1974, p. 134.
4 *Proc. Brit. Acad.* XLV, 1959, p. 25.
5 N. T. de Grummond, *Archaeology*, XXX, 1977, p. 14.
6 J. de Seznec, *Essais sur Diderot et l'Antiquité*, Oxford 1957.
7 R. F. Jones, *The Seventeenth Century*, Stanford 1951, p. 10.
8 Piggott, *Ruins in a Landscape*, Chap. VI.
9 *Ibid.*, p. 103.

10 Bernard Smith, *European Vision and the South Pacific*, Oxford 1960.
11 R. Tyler, *Francis Place* (Exhibition Catalogue), York 1971.
12 *Op. cit.* p. 71.
13 Piggott, *Ruins in a Landscape*, p. 111.
14 *Ibid.*, p. 118.
15 Louis Hawes, *Constable's Stonehenge* (Victoria and Albert Museum), London 1975, p. 12.
16 Bernard Smith *op. cit.* p. 51.
17 Ronald Jessup, *Man of Many Talents*, London 1975.
18 Harry Carter, *Orlando Jewitt: Wood Engraver*, London 1962, p. 5.
19 Piggott, *Antiq.* XXXIX, 1965, p. 174.

LIST OF ILLUSTRATIONS

4 Pentre Ifan burial chamber, Pembrokeshire. From George Owen's
manuscript *History of Pembrokeshire*,
1603. British Library, London, Ms
Harley 6250, f. 97 (101 of new
numbering).

5 Stonehenge. From William
Camden's *Britannia*, 1600.

6 John Aubrey (1626–97). Stonehenge, 1666. Pen-and-wash drawing after Inigo Jones. For John
Aubrey's *Monumenta Britannica*. Bodleian Library, Oxford, Ms. Top.
Gen., C. 24, f. 613.

7 Stonehenge. From Inigo Jones, *The
most notable Antiquity of Great Britain,
vulgarly called Stone-Heng .... Re-
stored, by Inigo Jones, Esq., Architect
General to the King*, 1655.

8 Views of Stonehenge, from west
and south, *c*.1675–1700. Engraving
by David Loggan. By courtesy of
the Salisbury and South Wiltshire
Museum, Salisbury. Crown Copy-
right, reproduced with permission
of the Controller of Her Majesty's
Stationery Office.

9 Ste Geneviève. French sixteenth-
century painting. Church of St
Merry, Paris. Photo Giraudon.

10 The Parthenon. Drawing by Giuliano da Sangallo, 1436, after Cyriac
of Ancona (1391–*c*.1455). Vatican
Library, Codex Barberinianus, f.
28v.

11 Peter Paul Rubens (1577–1640).
Gemma Tiberiana, 1622. Drawing.
Stedelijk Prentenkabinet, Antwerp.
Photo A C L, Brussels.

12 *Gemma Tiberiana*. First-century
cameo set in fourteenth-century
reliquary from Ste-Chapelle, Paris.
Cabinet des Medailles, Bibliothèque Nationale, Paris. Photo
Giraudon.

13 Samian sherds. From Comte de
Caylus, *Recueil d'antiquités*, Vol. 2,
1752–67.

14 John White (fl. 1585–93). Indian
village of Pomeiooc, Virginia,
c.1585–90. Watercolour. British
Museum, London.

15 Mesozoic fossils. From Martin Lister, *Historia animalium angliae*, 1678.

16 Frederik Ruysch's *Anatomisch Kab-
inet*. Engraving from his *Alle ontleed-
genees- en heelkundige werken, 2e deel*,
1744.

17 Prehistoric implements, figurine
and Early Christian crosses. From
Robert Plot, *Natural History of
Staffordshire*, 1686.

18 Charles Rennie Mackintosh
(1868–1928). Larkspur, Walber-
swick, 1914. Watercolour and pencil. Hunterian Art Gallery, University of Glasgow, Mackintosh
Collection.

19 Charles Rennie Mackintosh
(1868–1928). Cobbler's Cottage,
Holy Island, 1906. Pencil. Hunterian Art Gallery, University of
Glasgow, Mackintosh Collection.

20 Implements. From Robert Sibbald,
*Miscellanea quaedam cruditae anti-
quitatis*, 1710.

21 Pots. From Robert Sibbald, *Miscellanea quaedam eruditae antiquitatis*,
1710.

22 Disc-brooch from Sutton, Isle of
Ely. Drawing by George Hickes for
*Linguarum Veterum Septentrionalium
Thesaurus*, 1705.

22 Engraved silver disc-brooch found
at Sutton, Isle of Ely. Eleventh
century. British Museum, London.

23 Ascribed to Francis Place
(1647–1728). York Minster, *c*.1710.
Wash drawing. York City Art
Gallery.

24 John Aubrey (1626–97). Romanesque and early Gothic windows from Kington St Michael church, Wiltshire, Kemp Hall, Oxford, and St Giles church, Oxford. From John Aubrey's unpublished *Chronologia Architectonica, c.*1670. Bodleian Library, Oxford, Ms. Top. Gen.C. 25, f. 155.

25 John Aubrey (1626–97). Avebury. From his unpublished *Monumenta Britannica, c.*1675. Bodleian Library, Oxford, Ms. Top. Gen. C. 24, f. 39 v–40.

26 William Stukeley (1687–1765). Avebury, 1724. From William Stukeley, *Abury*, 1743.

27 Y Garn Fawr, Llandwnda, Pembrokeshire. Plan made for Edward Lhwyd by William Jones, 1697–8. British Library, London, Ms Stowe 1024, f. 43v.

28 Y Garn Fawr, Llanwnda, Pembrokeshire. Plan by W. F. Grimes, 1932.

29 Roman camp near Kirkboddo. From William Roy, *The Military Antiquities of the Romans in North Britain*, 1773.

30 Roman 'distance slab' from Bridgeness. National Museum of Antiquities, Edinburgh.

31 Roman 'distance slab' from Bridgeness. Engraving from John Horsley, *Brittania Romana*, 1732.

32 Roman mosaic pavement, Littlecote, Wiltshire. Engraving by George Vertue, 1730. Photo Ashmolean Museum, Oxford.

33 Beaker and associated grave goods in their own landscape at Winterslow, 1814. Painting by Mr Guest of Salisbury. Salisbury and South Wiltshire Museum, Salisbury.

34 Siberian jewellery. From N. C. Witsen, *Noord en Oost Tartarye*, 1785.

35 Anglo-Saxon antiquities. From James Douglas, *Nenia Britannica*, 1793.

36 Pentre Ifan chambered tomb, Pembrokeshire, *c.*1830. By courtesy of the Society of Antiquaries of London.

37 William Hodges (1744–97). Easter Island statues, after 1774. National Maritime Museum – on loan from Ministry of Defence (Navy).

38 Portions of shields from the Thames near Wandsworth. Lithograph by Orlando Jewitt. From J. M. Kemble and A. W. Franks, *Horae Ferales*, 1863.

39 Plan of Barrow 27, Handley Down. From A. H. L. Pitt-Rivers, *Excavations in Cranborne Chase*, 1887.

40 Camps on Hambledon Hill. From Heywood Sumner, (1853–1940) *Ancient Earthworks of Cranborne Chase*, 1913.

41 Plan of Maiden Castle by R. E. M. Wheeler and Huntly S. Gordon, 1934–7. From R. E. M. Wheeler, *Maiden Castle, Dorset*, 1943.

42 Plan of Hambledon Hill. From Heywood Sumner, *Ancient Earthworks of Cranborne Chase*, 1913.